D0833973

GRAHAM HARVEY

Who's Who in The Archers

2011

1 3 5 7 9 10 8 6 4 2

This book is published to accompany the BBC Radio 4 serial The Archers. The editor of The Archers is Vanessa Whitburn.

Published in 2010 by BBC Books, an imprint of Ebury Publishing. A Random House Group Company.

Main text by Graham Harvey
Copyright © Woodlands Books 2010

The Random House Group Limited Reg. No. 954009.
Addresses for companies within the Random House Group can be found at www.randomhouse.co.uk

A CIP catalogue record for this book is available from the British Library.

ISBN 978 1 849 90015 7

The Random House Group Limited supports The Forest Stewardship Council (FSC), the leading international forest certification organisation. All our titles that are printed on Greenpeace approved FSC certified paper carry the FSC logo. Our paper procurement policy can be found at www.rbooks.co.uk/environment

Commissioning editor: Albert DePetrillo
Project editor: Steve Tribe
Editorial manager: Nicholas Payne
Typeset in Garamond Light

Printed and bound in the UK by
CPI Mackays, Chatham ME5 8TD

Events in Ambridge are constantly changing, but we have done our best to make Who's Who in The Archers 2011 accurate at the time of publication.

Official Archers Website: bbc.co.uk/archers, to listen again to Archers episodes, including podcasts and an audio archive of the last seven days. The site also features daily plot synopses, news, information, a map of Ambridge, a detailed timeline, archive moments, quizzes and chat.

Official Fan Club: Archers Addicts www.archers-addicts.com

THE AUTHOR
Having spent his early career working as a farming journalist, Graham Harvey joined the script-writing team of The Archers in 1984. Almost 600 episodes later he took over as Agricultural Story Editor, a sort of Farm Minister for Ambridge. He considers it, quite simply, the best job in the world.

WELCOME TO AMBRIDGE

We're delighted to be back with the twelfth edition of our handy guide to the characters and locations in *The Archers*.

It has been another dramatic year in Ambridge, with Pip embarking on an ill-fated love affair, Lilian and Matt taking on Borchester Land in the property game and Helen deciding to become pregnant by donor insemination. And there have been yet more upheavals at The Bull.

This book will bring you fully up to date on these and other stories. We hope you'll enjoy it.

Vanessa Whitburn
Editor, *The Archers*

FREQUENTLY ASKED QUESTIONS

When and how can I hear the programme?
On BBC Radio 4 (92–95 FM, 198 LW and on digital radio and television). Transmission times: 7pm Sunday to Friday, repeated at 2pm the next day, excluding Saturdays. An omnibus edition of the whole week's episodes is broadcast every Sunday at 10am. It can also be heard worldwide via podcasts or the BBC iPlayer (go to the Archers website: bbc.co.uk/archers).

How many people listen?
Nearly five million every week in the UK alone. The Archers is the most popular non-news programme on BBC Radio 4, and the most-listened-to BBC programme online.

How long has it been going?
Five pilot episodes were broadcast on the BBC Midlands Home Service in Whit Week 1950, but The Archers' first national broadcast was on 1 January 1951. Episode 15,908 went out on 1 October 2009, making this comfortably the world's longest-running drama series.

How did it start?

The creator of The Archers, Godfrey Baseley, devised the programme as a means of educating farmers in modern production methods when Britain was still subject to food rationing.

So it's an educational programme?

Not any more. The Archers lost its original educational remit in the early 1970s – but it still prides itself on the quality of its research and its reflection of real rural life.

How is it planned and written?

The Editor, Vanessa Whitburn, leads a ten-strong production team and nine writers as they plot the complicated lives of the families in Ambridge, looking ahead months or sometimes years in biannual long-term meetings. The detailed planning is done at monthly script meetings about two months ahead of transmission. Each writer produces a week's worth of scripts in a remarkable 13 days.

... and recorded?

Actors receive their scripts a few days before recording, which takes place every four weeks in a state-of-the-art studio at the BBC's premises in the Mailbox complex in central Birmingham. Twenty-four episodes are recorded digitally in six intensive days, using only two hours of studio time per thirteen-minute episode. This schedule means that being an Archers actor is by no means a full-time job, even for major characters, so many also have careers in film, theatre, television or other radio drama.

What's that 'dum-di-dum' tune?

The Archers' signature tune is a 'maypole dance': 'Barwick Green', from the suite My Native Heath by Yorkshire composer Arthur Wood.

How did you get that news item in?

Episodes are transmitted three to six weeks after recording. But listeners are occasionally intrigued to hear topical events reflected in that evening's broadcast, a feat achieved through a flurry of rewriting, re-recording and editing on the day of transmission.

CHARACTERS BY FORENAME

The characters in this book are listed alphabetically by surname or nickname. If you only know the forename, this should help you locate the relevant entry.

Abbie Tucker
Adam Macy
Alan Franks
Alice Carter
Alistair Lloyd
Amy Franks
Annabelle Schrivener
Annette Turner
Ben Archer
Bert Fry
Brenda Tucker
Brian Aldridge
Bunty and Reg Hebden
Caroline Sterling
Christine Barford
Christopher Carter
Clarrie Grundy
Clive Horrobin
Coriander Snell
Daniel Hebden Lloyd
David Archer
Debbie Aldridge
Deepak Gupta
Ed Grundy
Eddie Grundy
Elizabeth Pargetter
Emma Grundy
Fallon Rogers
Freda Fry
George Grundy
Graham Ryder
Harry Mason

Hayley Tucker
Hazel Woolley
Heather Pritchard
Helen Archer
Ian Craig
Izzy Blake
Jack Woolley
Jake Hanson
James Bellamy
Jamie Perks
Jazzer McCreary
Jennifer Aldridge
Jill Archer
Jim Lloyd
Joe Grundy
Jolene Perks
Josh Archer
Jude Simpson
Kate Madikane
Kathy Perks
Kenton Archer
Kirsty Miller
Leonie Snell
Lewis Carmichael
Lilian Bellamy
Lily and Freddie
  Pargetter
Lorna Gibbs
Lucas Madikane
Lynda Snell
Mabel Thompson
Matt Crawford

Maurice Horton
Mike Tucker
Mia Hanson
Neil Carter
Nic Hanson
Nigel Pargetter
Oliver Sterling
Pat Archer
Patrick Hennessey
Paul Morgan
Peggy Woolley
Phoebe Aldridge
Pip Archer
Rachel Dorsey
Robert Snell
Roy Tucker
Ruairi Donovan
Ruth Archer
Sabrina and Richard
  Thwaite
Satya Khanna
Shiv Gupta
Shula Hebden Lloyd
Stephen Chalkman
Susan Carter
Ted Griffiths
Tom Archer
Tony Archer
Usha Franks
Vicky Tucker
Wayne Tucson
William Grundy

Some can also be found under 'Silent Characters'

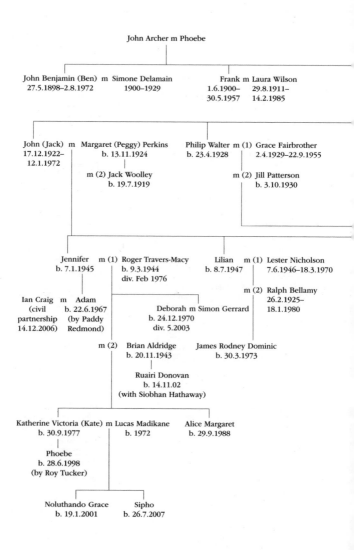

John Archer m Phoebe

John Benjamin (Ben) m Simone Delamain
27.5.1898–2.8.1972   1900–1929

Frank m Laura Wilson
1.6.1900–   29.8.1911–
30.5.1957   14.2.1985

John (Jack) m Margaret (Peggy) Perkins
17.12.1922–   b. 13.11.1924
12.1.1972

m (2) Jack Woolley
b. 19.7.1919

Philip Walter m (1) Grace Fairbrother
b. 23.4.1928   2.4.1929–22.9.1955

m (2) Jill Patterson
b. 3.10.1930

Jennifer   m (1) Roger Travers-Macy
b. 7.1.1945   b. 9.3.1944
div. Feb 1976

Lilian   m (1) Lester Nicholson
b. 8.7.1947   7.6.1946–18.3.1970

m (2) Ralph Bellamy
26.2.1925–
18.1.1980

Ian Craig   m   Adam
(civil   b. 22.6.1967
partnership   (by Paddy
14.12.2006)   Redmond)

Deborah m Simon Gerrard
b. 24.12.1970
div. 5.2003

m (2)   Brian Aldridge
b. 20.11.1943

James Rodney Dominic
b. 30.3.1973

Ruairi Donovan
b. 14.11.02
(with Siobhan Hathaway)

Katherine Victoria (Kate) m Lucas Madikane
b. 30.9.1977   b. 1972

Alice Margaret
b. 29.9.1988

Phoebe
b. 28.6.1998
(by Roy Tucker)

Noluthando Grace
b. 19.1.2001

Sipho
b. 26.7.2007

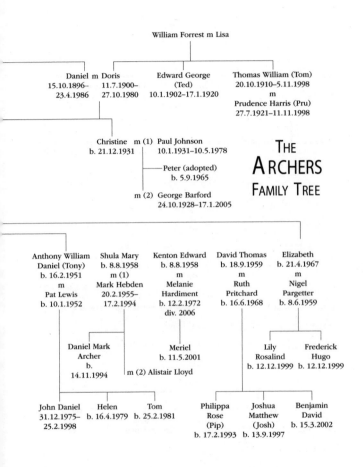

THE
ARCHERS
FAMILY TREE

William Forrest m Lisa

Daniel m Doris
15.10.1896–
23.4.1986

11.7.1900–
27.10.1980

Edward George
(Ted)
10.1.1902–17.1.1920

Thomas William (Tom)
20.10.1910–5.11.1998
m
Prudence Harris (Pru)
27.7.1921–11.11.1998

Christine m (1) Paul Johnson
b. 21.12.1931   10.1.1931–10.5.1978

Peter (adopted)
b. 5.9.1965

m (2) George Barford
24.10.1928–17.1.2005

Anthony William
Daniel (Tony)
b. 16.2.1951
m
Pat Lewis
b. 10.1.1952

Shula Mary
b. 8.8.1958
m (1)
Mark Hebden
20.2.1955–
17.2.1994

Kenton Edward
b. 8.8.1958
m
Melanie
Hardiment
b. 12.2.1972
div. 2006

David Thomas
b. 18.9.1959
m
Ruth
Pritchard
b. 16.6.1968

Elizabeth
b. 21.4.1967
m
Nigel
Pargetter
b. 8.6.1959

Daniel Mark
Archer
b.
14.11.1994

Meriel
b. 11.5.2001

m (2) Alistair Lloyd

Lily
Rosalind
b. 12.12.1999

Frederick
Hugo
b. 12.12.1999

John Daniel
31.12.1975–
25.2.1998

Helen
b. 16.4.1979

Tom
b. 25.2.1981

Philippa
Rose
(Pip)
b. 17.2.1993

Joshua
Matthew
(Josh)
b. 13.9.1997

Benjamin
David
b. 15.3.2002

BRIAN ALDRIDGE

Home Farm • Born 20.11.43

(Charles Collingwood)

Brian's uncanny gift for emerging from virtually any situation better off than before shows no sign of diminishing. His long-running affair with Siobhan Donovan, whose tragic death left him with a young son to care for, would have split many marriages. Yet, after all the traumas, Brian and **Jennifer** seem as strong as ever. Then there's Brian's boardroom battle with the business mogul **Matt Crawford**. The outcome of that was a conviction for fraud and a prison term for Matt, and Brian's elevation to chairman of the **Borchester Land** board. Though he has handed over control of Home Farm to stepdaughter **Debbie** and stepson **Adam Macy**, he's now running another sizeable chunk of England – the former Berrow **Estate**. There's no doubting Brian's business acumen, but his other great gift is his undeniable charm. He's as comfortable discussing pheasant poults with gamekeeper **William Grundy** as he is swapping stories with the Borsetshire *glitterati* at a charity ball at **Lower Loxley**.

DEBBIE ALDRIDGE

(née Travers-Macy, formerly Gerrard)
Home Farm • Born 24.12.70
(Tamsin Greig)

Since moving to a farm in Hungary – another of her stepfather **Brian**'s business interests – Debbie has been just an occasional visitor to Ambridge. Even so, she manages to make her influence felt at **Home Farm**, running the arable enterprise by email from across the Danube. It's an arrangement that her brother and farming partner **Adam Macy** – who's on the receiving end of most of these missives – is not entirely happy with. These days she's getting on better with Brian, whose philandering with Siobhan Donovan left her hurt and angry. There's no doubt of his admiration for her farm management skills, which are now bearing fruit in Eastern Europe. She in turn is impressed by his plans to develop a big new livestock market through **Borchester Land**. Ambition is a quality they both share.

JENNIFER ALDRIDGE

(née Archer, formerly Travers-Macy)
Home Farm • Born 7.1.45
(Angela Piper)

Family has always been at the centre of Jennifer's life. Her son **Adam** (now **Macy**) was born in 1967 following her affair with a local cowman. Daughter **Debbie** was born during her marriage to Roger Travers-Macy, who adopted Adam. The marriage didn't last, and in 1976 Jennifer married **Brian Aldridge**, with whom she had two daughters: **Kate** (now **Madikane**) and **Alice** (now **Carter**). Much later – and after a great deal of mental anguish – Jennifer agreed to make a home for Brian's illegitimate son **Ruairi Donovan**. It's a measure of her strength that she held the family together through the ensuing upheavals. More recently, there have been plenty of events to test Jennifer's resilience, not least the continued decline of her stepfather **Jack Woolley**, who has Alzheimer's. She has also been called upon to support her sister **Lilian** while her beloved **Matt Crawford** was serving a prison sentence for fraud.

PHOEBE ALDRIDGE

Willow Farm • Born 28.6.98
(Lucy Morris)

Though Phoebe lives with **Roy** and **Hayley Tucker**, her real mum is **Kate Madikane**, now living in South Africa. Phoebe was born in a tepee at Glastonbury Festival while Kate was living the life of a happy hippy, despite her relationship with the clean-cut, home-loving Roy. When Kate moved to Johannesburg, care of Phoebe was taken over by Roy and Hayley, with doting grandmother **Jennifer** in close support. Phoebe is growing up fast and is getting on well at Borchester Green secondary school. She has a half-sister **Abbie Tucker**, and is part of a settled, loving family, well rooted in the Ambridge village community. Now the exotic Kate is back to study international development at **Felpersham** University and Phoebe could be in for a rocky ride.

It's what estate agents call 'a highly sought-after village'. Plenty of desirable properties, a village pond, a pub (**The Bull**), a gently meandering river (the Am), and a village shop, newly converted to a **community shop**. There's a pleasant market town within easy commuting distance and, if you fancy a day's shopping in Birmingham, you can get a train from **Hollerton Junction** just a few miles away. There's another phrase you might find on the estate agent's blurb: Ambridge is what they like to call 'an active village community'. Which either means there's plenty going on or there's always someone trying to cajole you into something you'd much rather stay out of, depending on your point of view. Sadly, the village is not entirely free of twenty-first-century problems. Just recently there's been an outbreak of spray-paint graffiti around the place.

AMBRIDGE COMMUNITY SHOP

For years the village shop was owned by businessman **Jack Woolley.** But with Jack now suffering from Alzheimer's, his wife **Peggy** decided to put the shop on the market, threatening its future. That's when a group of enterprising locals set out to turn it into a community resource. The group includes **Pat Archer**, **Kathy Perks**, Richard Thwaite, **Usha Franks**, **Susan Carter**, **Lynda Snell**, **Brian Aldridge**, **David Archer** and **Oliver Sterling**. Peggy supported the plan by leasing the shop at a peppercorn rent. The idea is to run it with mostly volunteer labour and, where possible, to sell a range of local foods. Whether ultimately the Community Shop succeeds or fails, it's unarguable that **Ambridge** is giving it a good go. **Helen Archer** lives in a small flat above the shop.

AMBRIDGE GOLF CLUB

In the local tourist guides it's listed as a challenging nine-hole course within a beautiful parkland setting. Originally part of Grey Gables, it was sold to land-and-property company **Borchester Land** in 2006, along with the country park. Under its director of golf, Leigh Barham, the club has grown in popularity in recent years. Clubhouse catering manager **Kathy Perks**, who took over in 2008, has greatly extended the restaurant menu making it a notable lunch venue. It's a facility greatly enjoyed by **Lilian Bellamy**, who has even been known to play an occasional round. She is sometimes accompanied by her sister **Jennifer**, and occasionally by her partner **Matt Crawford**. This is a welcome return for Matt, who for many months never visited the club. The reason for his absence was never spoken of in the clubhouse.

AMBRIDGE HALL

Featured in the local tourist board publication *Borsetshire's Best B & Bs*, Ambridge Hall must be one of the most relaxing guest houses in the area thanks to hostess **Lynda Snell**'s powers of feng shui. No effort has been spared in creating an atmosphere that is at once restful and yet stimulating. Outside there's a charming patio of Welsh slate (designed by the owner and built by local craftsmen) and beyond that a delightful, mature garden with an intriguing 'low-allergen' area, specially created by the owner who suffers from hay fever. The gardens run down to the River Am where, according to the owner, kingfishers and otters can sometimes be seen. Alongside the garden there's a small grass paddock where visitors can meet Ambridge Hall's resident llamas – Constanza, Wolfgang and Salieri.

AMBRIDGE ORGANICS

Harcourt Road, Borchester

Designed to bring the 'farm shop experience into the centre of town', Ambridge Organics is an offshoot of local organic farmers, **Bridge Farm** of Ambridge. Set up by farmers **Pat** and **Tony Archer**, it's managed by their daughter **Helen**, whose well-known cheeses are sold in the shop. Also employed in the shop are Anja, from Poland, and **Kirsty Miller**. Like many organic retail businesses, Ambridge Organics has had a difficult time due to the recession. However, its mix of ethical and locally sourced vegetables, salads, meats, dairy products and speciality foods has helped maintain a loyal core of committed customers.

BEN ARCHER

Brookfield Farm • Born 15.3.02

(Thomas Lester)

Coming so soon after **Ruth**'s treatment for breast cancer, Ben's arrival at **Brookfield Farm** was a special blessing. **David** and Ruth have to remind themselves of this when young Ben's in the middle of a noisy squabble with his elder siblings **Josh** and **Pip**, or when he's complaining about how unfair it is that he's not allowed the same freedoms as they are simply because he's younger.

DAVID ARCHER

Brookfield Farm • Born 18.9.59

(Timothy Bentinck)

When he hit 50, David – devoted family man and farmer – thought he'd got his life just about as he wanted it. On the farm he'd made the business pretty much recession-proof by putting the dairy herd on a low-cost, paddock grazing system and by building up the direct-selling beef operation. He'd even allowed himself more time off the farm, becoming actively involved in the local NFU. But if he thought he was in for a quieter life he had reckoned without the impact of a teenage daughter. **Pip**'s relationship with **Jude Simpson**, a student twelve years her senior, shattered any illusions he had of himself as a modern, tolerant father. In an earlier age, he'd probably have had the man horsewhipped. As **Ruth** pointed out, it probably wasn't the best state of mind for dealing with the situation. In a further blow, David lost his father, the widely respected Phil Archer, in February 2010.

HELEN ARCHER

Above the village shop • Born 16.4.79

(Louiza Patikas)

In the school of hard knocks, **Pat** and **Tony Archer**'s daughter has taken a bigger bashing than most. First she lost two of the men most important in her life – her brother John in a tractor accident and, a few years later, her partner Greg Turner, who committed suicide. Her unhappiness led to anorexia, then to a non-stop round of drinking and partying. After a spell of counselling she began to put her life back together, taking the small flat above the village shop. The arrival of Greg's young daughter, **Annette Turner**, seemed to add a new purpose to life, but when the girl left quickly following an abortion, Helen once more faced a broken relationship. From her sadness sprang a determination to have a child of her own by sperm donation. It was a decision that shocked her father Tony, who did his best to change her mind. But her mother Pat offered her full support.

JILL ARCHER

(née Patterson)
Glebe Cottage • Born 3.10.30
(Patricia Greene)

For Jill, devoted wife and mother, 2010 will be remembered as the year she lost her beloved Phil. Just three years after the couple celebrated their golden wedding anniversary, she returned from a trip out with family members to find that he'd died peacefully in his armchair. In their sadness the children – **Kenton**, **Shula** (now **Hebden Lloyd**), **David** and **Elizabeth** (now **Pargetter**) – gathered round to comfort Jill. Many outside the immediate family also rallied in support, such was the respect she and Phil were held in. Despite her grief, no one doubts Jill's strength and ability to carry on. She'll continue to play a role at the heart of family and village life, that much is certain. She'll also go on speaking out on issues she cares about, such as hunting. For that is the nature of this stalwart countrywoman.

JOSH ARCHER

Brookfield Farm • Born 13.9.97

(Cian Cheesbrough)

David and **Ruth**'s middle child has begun to show the early signs of teenage rebellion. He was found to have been involved in an outbreak of spray-paint graffiti around the village, an offence for which he was grounded and given extra tasks by his worried parents. Despite this Josh remains an amiable boy, well liked at **Borchester** Green secondary school. At home he's started to be useful around the farm. Like his big sister **Pip**, he seems to be a born farmer. He has always been fond of animals and is good with the cows. He has also got a strong entrepreneurial streak which David and Ruth hope will channel his energies in a more productive direction than street art.

KENTON ARCHER

April Cottage • Born 8.8.58

(Richard Attlee)

Kenton's grand plan to bring smart café society to sleepy old **Borchester** has come at a cost. With the backing of **Jim Lloyd**, he has transformed the homely comforts of **Jaxx** Caff into a sophisticated watering hole for young, upwardly mobile professionals. But his preoccupation with the project led to a widening rift with his partner **Kathy Perks**. After a series of rows and upsets – including his crashing out overnight on **Kirsty Miller**'s sofa – Kenton and Kathy separated. He moved into **Lower Loxley**, where his presence had a bad influence on his brother-in-law, **Nigel Pargetter**. Whether Kenton can repair the rift with Kathy looks increasingly uncertain.

PAT ARCHER

(née Lewis)
Bridge Farm • Born 10.1.52
(Patricia Gallimore)

Pat believes in good food for everyone. This is why she and husband **Tony** converted **Bridge Farm** to organic and started marketing their own dairy products. It's also why she worked hard to establish the Transition Towns movement in **Ambridge**. Pat, the lifelong green activist, wants to see a new food movement based on local produce. She's delighted that her son **Tom** has returned to the family farm and is working towards the same goal. But for all her grandiose ideas, Pat remains first and foremost a loving mother. Seeing daughter **Helen** suffer so much unhappiness in her life has been difficult for Pat. Now Helen is intent on bringing up a baby on her own, she's determined to give her daughter every bit of support and help she can.

PIP ARCHER

Brookfield Farm • Born 17.2.93

(Helen Monks)

David and **Ruth Archer**'s eldest child seemed ideally suited to life on the farm. Even as a small child she enjoyed working with the animals, and now as a teenager she is a skilled milker. She's an enthusiastic member of the local Young Farmers branch, and chose to do a diploma in environmental science in addition to her A levels at **Borchester** College. She's keenly interested in the wildlife at **Brookfield**, particularly the barn owls. But the earnest teenager's relationship with a fellow-student twelve years her senior caused ructions in the family home. Jude's influence disrupted her exams, so she has to retake some of her AS Levels in January 2011. However, the ill-fated romance is behind her and she's looking to the future.

RUTH ARCHER

(née Pritchard)
Brookfield Farm • Born 16.6.68
(Felicity Finch)

The regular milker at **Brookfield Farm**, Ruth has played a key role in making the dairy herd the efficient, grass-based operation it has now become. Though this Northumberland girl felt something of an outsider when she first arrived in **Ambridge**, the farm and the people of the village have become central to her life. After her recovery from breast cancer – and a brief affair with herdsman Sam Batton – she's all too aware that she could easily have lost everything. Such life-changing experiences have made her a little less dogmatic than **David** in the way they care for their children, **Pip**, **Josh** and **Ben**. So when Pip's love affair with an older man provoked a mood of angry confrontation in David, Ruth preferred to be more circumspect. Not surprisingly Ruth's softly-softly approach won the day.

TOM ARCHER

1, The Green • Born 25.2.81

(Tom Graham)

Sometimes Tom's ambition to become a major player in the quality foods industry is let down by some rather flaky business decisions. Such as when he entered a brief and ill-fated affair with a supermarket buyer, only to find his product de-listed when the relationship ended. Today, Tom's a wiser man. After an uneasy business partnership with his uncle, **Brian Aldridge**, he moved his pig production business back to the security of the family organic farm. He also got engaged to **Brenda Tucker** and urged her to get wed. But Brenda had other ideas, choosing to build a career in marketing first. She took a job in Leicester involving a daily commute of four hours. Life is easier now she has taken a job in Ambridge, though Tom isn't delighted that she has chosen to work with **Lilian Bellamy** and **Matt Crawford**. He doesn't think the decision bodes well for her future.

TONY ARCHER

Bridge Farm • Born 16.2.51

(Colin Skipp)

Tony is known as a bit of a whinger. But then he'd say he had plenty to whinge about. He and his wife **Pat** have built up a successful organic farm and food business. Yet here he is pushing 60 and still hand-pulling leeks and attaching teat cups to cows' udders. Plus he has a bigger mortgage than ever now he and Pat have bought up the tenancy of the farm so they can hand it on to their kids, **Helen** and **Tom**. What really shook Tony's ordered world was Helen's decision to have a child by donor insemination. His view that she'd be much better off waiting for the right man to come along really got up her nose. It remains to be seen whether he'll support her when the baby arrives.

CHRISTINE BARFORD

(née Archer, formerly Johnson)
Woodbine Cottage • Born 21.12.31
(Lesley Saweard)

Having run the riding stables for many years, Phil Archer's younger sister Chris sold up to her niece **Shula Hebden Lloyd** and settled down to a quiet retirement. She sees little of Peter, her adopted son by her first marriage, who travels widely as an administrator with a symphony orchestra. Her second marriage to solid, dependable gamekeeper George Barford ended tragically when he died shortly after their house was fire-bombed. Arsonist **Clive Horrobin** got twelve years for his crime. Chris now hopes to see out her days quietly. In 2008 she became a churchwarden at **St Stephen's**.

JAMES BELLAMY

Born 30.3.73

(Roger May)

Lilian **Bellamy**'s son, whose intermittent appearances in Ambridge coincide with any concerns he has about losing his inheritance. The last time he called to see his dear old mum was on her birthday following a temporary separation from her partner **Matt Crawford**. Ever the protective son, James called on Matt and warned him off. Whether this was in his mother's interests or his own is open to conjecture.

LILIAN BELLAMY

(née Archer, formerly Nicholson)
The Dower House • Born 8.7.47
(Sunny Ormonde)

The former good-time girl with a taste for gin – now the devoted partner of property developer and general wheeler-dealer **Matt Crawford** – 'stood by her man' while he served a gaol sentence for fraud. Dutifully she visited him in his open prison, tactfully defusing his anger and frustrations at life inside. But Lilian's no rug for her 'Tiger' to walk on. When Matt suggested she set up a property business for him to run behind the scenes following his release, she was determined to set a few ground rules first. For a start she was to be no 'sleeping partner'. She would take a full part in the decision making, she insisted. While Matt was inside, Lilian found unexpected support and comfort in the shape of his half-brother, builder **Paul Morgan**. Though the relationship never became physical, Matt felt sufficiently threatened to warn Paul off when he was finally released under a Home Detention Curfew.

IZZY BLAKE

Meadow Rise, Borchester • Born 1993
(Lizzie Wofford)

Pip Archer's best friend from **Borchester** Green school, Izzy had no intention of following her to Borchester College for an A level course. Izzy isn't interested in delayed gratification – she wants the good times now. This means following in her mother's footsteps and working on the supermarket checkout. Despite their differing pathways, the two girls remained good friends. Izzy knew all about Pip's older man long before **Ruth** and **David Archer** heard the shocking news. In fact it was Izzy who let the cat out of the bag about Jude Simpson's true age. Not that Izzy wanted to make trouble for her friend. It's just that, like Pip, she didn't see the 'age thing' as an issue.

BORCHESTER

While most of the tourists head for the more glitzy city of **Felpersham**, this market town on the banks of the River Am has its own subdued charm. Alongside the Old Wool Market (now up-market apartments), there's a part-pedestrianised shopping centre that still retains some attractive shop-fronts. There are the usual multiples, of course, but among them a few individual, even quirky, retailers still survive. Underwoods, the town's own department store, remains a favourite destination. Among the smaller businesses is the refurbished **Jaxx** café-bar in Oriel Road, and **Ambridge Organics** in Harcourt Road. Entertainments include a multiplex cinema, the Theatre Royal, the municipal leisure centre and swimming pool. For those seeking the outdoor life, the town's information centre displays a poster proclaiming: 'Borchester – Gateway to the Hassett Hills'.

BORCHESTER LAND

With his deft move into the chairman's seat during an ill-tempered boardroom tussle, **Brian Aldridge** did nothing to dull his reputation as one of the sharpest business operators around. Anyone who thought that by handing over the day-to-day running of **Home Farm** to his stepson **Adam** he might be planning to take things quieter will have had a rude awakening. This master tactician now finds himself in effective control of one of the largest blocks of land in south **Borsetshire**, including the former Berrow **Estate**. No one expects him to be content with farming it. BL's principal aim is to maximise the value of its real estate assets, which means looking for development opportunities wherever they exist. Aldridge and his fellow board member **Annabelle Schrivener**, the company lawyer, are unlikely to forget this. The company's assets in Ambridge include the pheasant shoot, run by head keeper **Will Grundy**, and the business units at Sawyer's Farm.

BORSETSHIRE

A largely rural county of gently undulating farmlands and meandering rivers, a pleasant if unspectacular landscape made much of by the regional tourist board. However, the county boasts a fine range of hills – the Hassetts – which are becoming increasingly popular with walkers. The charming cathedral city of **Felpersham**, with its art gallery and museum, stands in the east of the county with the bustling market town of **Borchester** to the north. The county's two main newspapers – the *Felpersham Advertiser* and the *Borchester Echo* – have so far both survived the slump in advertising revenue, though with much reduced staffs. Through it all, Radio Borsetshire appears to go from strength to strength. The attractive village of **Ambridge** lies south of Borchester, a few miles from the Hassett Hills.

BRIDGE FARM

LAND
140 acres owned plus 32 acres rented

STOCK
92 milking cows (Friesians) • 45 followers (heifers/calves)
45 fattening pigs

CROPS
115 acres grassland • 10 acres barley • 25 acres wheat • 5 acres potatoes • 4 acres carrots • 2 acres leeks • 3 acres Swedes • 2 acres Dutch cabbage • 1 acre Savoy cabbage • 5 acres mixed vegetable and salad crops, including two poly-tunnels

LABOUR
Tony Archer • **Pat Archer** • **Tom Archer** • **Helen Archer**
Jazzer McCreary (part-time, pigs)
Susan Carter (part-time, dairy) • **Clarrie Grundy** (dairy)

Tony and **Pat Archer** are delighted that, having taken on a sizeable mortgage to buy the freehold of their organic farm from **Borchester Land**, they are now seeing far more commitment to the family business from their son **Tom**. Not only has he brought his pig enterprise back to the family acres, he's lending his dad a hand in all sorts of ways, including milking. **Helen**'s commitment to the farm has always been rock solid, though no one's quite sure just yet how the new baby might change things. **Clarrie Grundy** works full-time in the dairy, with **Susan Carter** working part-time. One of the newer developments on the farm is the wetland ecosystem waste treatment area.

BROOKFIELD FARM

LAND
469 acres owned

STOCK
180 milking cows (Friesians) • 79 followers (heifers – some
Brown Swiss crosses) • 85 beef cattle (Herefords) • 350 ewes
few hens

CROPS
339 acres grassland • 88 acres cereals • 10 acres oilseed rape
10 acres potatoes • 12 acres beans • 10 acres forage maize

LABOUR
David Archer (managing) • **Ruth Archer** (dairy herd manager)
Eddie Grundy (relief herdsperson) • **Bert Fry** (retired, casual)
Biff (sheepdog)

With an eye to reducing costs and keeping the farm profitable, **David** and **Ruth** are operating a paddock grazing system for the dairy herd. High quality Hereford beef is sold online and at the farm gate, with lambs from the sheep flock being marketed co-operatively under the Hassett Hills brand. The arable acreage is managed on contract by **Home Farm**. David and Ruth's daughter **Pip** lends a hand on the farm when college work permits.

THE BULL

Once one of the most popular hostelries in south **Borsetshire**, its fortunes have taken a distinct dip since the death in New Zealand of popular landlord Sid Perks. Without her beloved Sid, his widow **Jolene** had no heart for running the place. The once cheerful atmosphere of the bar became a sombre one, and regulars started avoiding it. Jolene's daughter **Fallon Rogers** did her best to get things going again, with milkman **Harry Mason** in support. However, Jolene remained disconsolate and toyed with the idea of putting the pub on the market. A 'We Love The Bull' campaign started by Harry and the regulars may be helping to brighten things up.

LEWIS CARMICHAEL

Lower Loxley Hall
(Robert Lister)

The amiable Lewis, retired architect and all-round good egg, planned a rather more exciting life when he married **Nigel Pargetter**'s mother Julia at an age when most people are settling for a good book in the fireside armchair. The marriage – second time around for both of them – was destined to be a happy but brief one. Sadly, Julia died after just six months. These days Lewis – old family friend of the Pargetter family – amuses himself by lending an occasional hand in the Lower Loxley art gallery or tasting (professionally, of course) one of Nigel's Lower Loxley wines. As Elizabeth Archer once remarked: 'Every fine old house needs a Lewis around to worry about it.'

ALICE CARTER

Home Farm / Southampton University
Born 29.9.88

(Hollie Chapman)

Despite her two years away at university, Alice's romance with the hunky young farrier **Christopher Carter** showed no sign of running out of steam as her mother **Jennifer** had hoped. In fact from Jennifer's point of view things were about to get a good deal worse. The couple returned from a summer American road trip with the sensational news that they'd got married in Las Vegas. Though Jennifer was horrified, it was clear that Alice was blissfully happy. Bravely Jennifer organised a celebratory party for the happy couple with Christopher's parents – **Neil** and **Susan Carter** – supplying the cake – a multi-tiered creation with cupcakes. After the celebration, the couple enjoyed a brief spell of married bliss in Alice's cottage before she went back to Southampton to begin her final year at university.

CHRISTOPHER CARTER

Ambridge View • Born 22.6.88

(William Sanderson-Thwaite)

The hearts of most of **Ambridge**'s young females collectively sank when the news got round that hunk Chris Carter had returned from his American road trip married to his girlfriend **Alice**. Chris is widely admired for his rugged good looks and remarkable set of pecs. Though **Jennifer Aldridge** was less than ecstatic about the marriage, husband **Brian** was rather amused by it all. As he pointed out, their new son-in-law was welcomed by some of the poshest horse-owning families in the county. Meanwhile the amiable Chris appears unfazed by having married into Ambridge's biggest landowning family. His main concern is how he'll get by without his lovely new wife while she's finishing her degree at Southampton University.

NEIL CARTER

Ambridge View • Born 22.5.57
(Brian Hewlett)

Y ou could say that Neil and pigs were made for each other. Just be careful not to say it in front of Neil's wife **Susan.** She always wanted something better for her Neil – better meaning that you put a suit and tie on to go to work and didn't come home smelling of Gloucester Old Spots. Sadly she has had to acknowledge that Neil is never happier than when working with his pigs. He started as herdsmen at the late Phil Archer's pig unit at Hollowtree. These days he raises weaners from his own herd on his eight acres at **Willow Farm**, where he and Susan have built their own house. A bell-ringer – he's tower captain at **St Stephen's** – keen cricketer, churchwarden and chair of the Parish Council, Neil gets on with just about everybody. His daughter **Emma** is currently living with one-time tearaway, now dairy farmer **Ed Grundy**, while his son **Christopher** is married to successful landowner's daughter **Alice**.

SUSAN CARTER

(née Horrobin)
Ambridge View • Born 10.10.63
(Charlotte Martin)

Working in the village shop was the perfect job for Susan because, whatever happened in **Ambridge**, she got to know about it first. So news that **Peggy Woolley** was selling the shop came as a shock. Luckily, it has become a **Community Shop**, with Susan staying on as post mistress and chief stock controller. She enjoys the job, despite the unreliability of some of the volunteers. She's made up her hours by working part-time for **Pat Archer** at **Bridge Farm** Dairy. This came as a great relief, since her husband **Neil**'s organic pig enterprise has looked a bit rocky lately. A woman of strong social aspirations, Susan is delighted that son **Christopher** has married **Alice,** daughter of **Brian** and **Jennifer Aldridge**. She's less happy that daughter **Emma** has settled down with **Ed Grundy** having had a son by Ed's brother **Will**. Now Ed and Emma have a child of their own on the way, she's hoping that things will be more settled.

CASA NUEVA

The remote hideaway home of gamekeeper **Will Grundy** and his partner **Nic Hanson** along with her two children, **Jake** and **Mia**. The tied cottage is owned by Will's bosses, **Borchester Land**, owners of the **Estate**. Will once lived there with his first love **Emma Grundy** following the couple's return from their Mexican honeymoon, but the ill-fated marriage wasn't to last and Emma went off with Will's younger brother **Ed**. These days Will has found happiness at Casa Nueva with his new family. It's remote but handy for Will's shoot. Townee Nic is starting to get used to it now she has learnt to drive.

STEPHEN CHALKMAN

Borchester • Her Majesty's Prison

(Stephen Critchlow)

Matt Crawford's partner in crime picked up a far longer stretch for his part in the fraud. But then Matt cooperated in the police investigation while 'Chalky' disappeared 'on holiday'. A generally nasty piece of work, Chalky's not above threatening physical violence if he thinks it'll get him out of trouble. He tried the strong-arm methods on both **Brenda Tucker**, when she worked for Matt, and on **Lilian Bellamy**, Matt's partner. A former member of South **Borsetshire** District Council, he's no novice at 'white-collar crime'. He lost his seat on the council for failing to mention his wife's involvement in the planning application that led to the development of Grange Spinney, **Ambridge**. Like Matt, Chalkman was also on the board of **Borchester Land,** giving fellow board member **Brian Aldridge** a hard time for a while. He's now languishing in prison while Brian runs the board.

IAN CRAIG

Honeysuckle Cottage • Born 1970

(Stephen Kennedy)

The civil partner of farmer **Adam Aldridge**, Ian is delighted with life in Ambridge. He grew up in Northern Ireland, not noted for its tolerance of gay men. Now the easy-going chef of **Grey Gables** is happy to settle quietly into the social scene without feeling he has to make a big production of his sexuality, a notion that hasn't always been understood by Adam. Ian's disappointment at not fathering a child with his old friend Mads made him a good confidante to **Helen Archer** when she decided to have a baby by sperm donation. Listening to Helen's hopes and concerns raised a lot of ghosts for Ian, but it meant he could be there for her.

MATT CRAWFORD

The Dower House • Born 7.8.47
(Kim Durham)

Spending time in the 'slammer' for fraud came as a hefty blow to Matt. The self-made businessman and property developer from Peckham always considered himself smart enough to keep on the right side of the law when stitching together one of his iffy deals. But then he always considered himself a 'loner', too, well able to get by on his own wits. He didn't think he 'needed' anyone until **Lilian Bellamy** proved otherwise. Now out of prison, he's determined to climb back up the greasy pole using Lilian's money. But having stood by him through his trial and imprisonment, Lilian has no intention of making out a blank cheque. She's prepared to help him rebuild his empire, but she'll be alongside him every step of the way.

RUAIRI DONOVAN

Home Farm • Born 14.11.02

(Ciaran Coyle)

Ruairi is the boy who nearly ended the marriage of **Jennifer** and **Brian Aldridge**. The result of Brian's affair with Siobhan (Hathaway), he brought the boy back to **Home Farm** when his former mistress died of cancer in 2007. Despite the pain felt by Jennifer when she learned of the affair, she found the strength to give the boy the love and security he needed. Brian, too, embraced fatherhood again, giving up the day-to-day running of the farm to support Jennifer. Jennifer's anger at Brian was shared by her own offspring – **Debbie**, **Adam**, **Kate** and **Alice**. Slowly they are all adapting to the new reality of family life at Home Farm. If Jennifer has been strong enough to accept it, they can surely do no less.

RACHEL DORSEY

Felpersham

(Deborah McAndrew)

Like **Ambridge**'s vicar **Alan Franks**, the archdeacon of **Felpersham** diocese takes a modern, socially reformist view of Anglicanism. It was Rachel who supported him in his engagement and subsequent marriage to **Usha** (then Gupta), presiding over the marriage service in the summer of 2008. She is also supportive of his imaginative engagement with issues like social deprivation. To commemorate Christ's retreat to the wilderness, Alan spent Lent camping out at night to draw attention to – and raise money for – homeless people and refugees. Rachel is certain to have been one of his sponsors.

THE ESTATE

Originally called the Berrow Estate, the 1,020-acre arable block is now part of the land and property portfolio of **Borchester Land**.

FELPERSHAM

Just seventeen miles from Ambridge, this cathedral city is a top destination for a day's shopping or a good night out. With its regular market and late-night shopping day (Thursdays), Felpersham offers most of the big high street names and a good number of the classier ones. Gourmet eating places include the Quince Tree and a clutch of riverside gastro pubs and bistros. There's a large regional hospital with a highly rated A & E unit, plus an expanding university where **Roy Tucker** and his sister **Brenda** once went. In recent years, a number of high-tech companies have relocated to Felpersham from Birmingham and London, helping to give it an air of prosperity.

ALAN FRANKS

The Vicarage, Ambridge
(John Telfer)

In some ways Alan would seem better suited to a challenging urban parish, such is his concern for the socially and economically disadvantaged. For example, he was willing to spend Lent under canvas – during one of the coldest springs in living memory – in order to raise awareness (and money) for the homeless. At the same time he likes nothing better than roaring along Borsetshire's leafy lanes on his motorbike – not infrequently with his Hindu wife **Usha** on the back. Generally popular with his parishioners, he has sadly upset a few, among them the then longstanding churchwarden **Shula Hebden**. He would be the first to admit that her opposition to his marriage to a Hindu was not well handled on his part. She now worships at **Felpersham** Cathedral, a fact that still causes Alan some distress.

AMY FRANKS

The Vicarage, Ambridge • Born 1989

(Vinette Robinson)

Mixed-race Amy is the Reverend **Alan's** daughter by his first wife Catherine, who died in 1995. She holds strong views on a number of social issues, including a disapproval of the military, an attitude that led to a severe strain on her friendship with her one-time best friend **Alice Carter**, who once had thoughts of joining the RAF. In the event Alice went off to Southampton University while Amy moved to Manchester, where she qualified as a midwife. She now works at **Felpersham** Hospital. Amy is never slow in defending what she believes is right, even taking on her doughty grandmother **Mabel Thompson** when she opposed Alan's relationship with and subsequent marriage to **Usha**, a Hindu.

USHA FRANKS

(née Gupta)
The Vicarage, Ambridge • Born 17.6.62
(Souad Faress)

Hindu Usha's marriage to Church of England vicar **Alan Franks** has been challenging to say the least. From the start the match attracted angry criticism both from her own community and the village community she had become part of. One of **Ambridge**'s longstanding churchwardens – **Shula Hebden Lloyd** – resigned after making what appeared as critical comments in the *Borchester Echo*. Much of the criticism has now subsided, and Usha has become a stalwart supporter of Alan, even over some of his more outlandish undertakings, such as spending the whole of Lent under canvas to raise money for refugees and the homeless. However, Usha is far from being the stereotypical 'vicar's wife'. A qualified solicitor, she is a partner in local law firm Jefferson Crabtree. She has also made something of a name for herself locally as an accomplished marathon runner.

BERT FRY

Brookfield Bungalow • Born 1936

(Eric Allan)

Now retired, Bert is one of that lost breed of the British countryside – the general farmworker. In a working life spent on the land, he acquired an array of agrarian skills, many of which are no longer needed in an age of mechanisation and agrochemicals. Nevertheless Bert takes a real pride in his hard-won skills, missing no opportunity to talk about them whenever someone will listen, such as at the annual Open Farm Sunday at his former workplace **Brookfield Farm**. Bert also conducts guided tours at the local stately home, **Lower Loxley**, home of **Elizabeth** and **Nigel Pargetter**. There's one traditional skill that Bert still practises – ploughing. He's a regular in many of the local ploughing matches, always entering the class for vintage tractors using the ageing Massey Ferguson bought for the purpose by **David Archer**. Bert's also a stalwart cricket umpire turning out regularly for the Ambridge cricket team.

FREDA FRY

Brookfield Bungalow

Loyal partner of **Bert** for more than fifty years, Freda has become something of a local legend for her cooking at **The Bull**. There her homemade pies and casseroles have become renowned in the village and beyond. Following the death of pub landlord Sid Perks, business dropped off sharply as Sid's widow **Jolene** lost all interest. However, with Jolene forging a new friendship with pub regular **Kenton Archer**, business has begun to pick up and Freda's savoury pies are in demand again. In her own kitchen, Freda is unquestionably queen, devoting herself to making an array of jams and pickles that are highly sought after at the annual Flower and Produce Show. Otherwise Freda is happy being a 'private person', content to let Bert take the limelight with his talks and poetry, and at **Lower Loxley Hall** where he is a volunteer guide.

LORNA GIBBS

(Alison Belbin)

Catering manager at **Lower Loxley Hall**, Lorna took over from **Kathy Perks** and runs the Lower Loxley café and shop, where she is **Emma Grundy**'s boss. She helps occasionally with village events, and once did the make-up for the village Christmas panto. Also known to have a good sense of humour, she once joined Kathy in playing an April Fool trick on Kenton Archer concerning the true meaning of his new tattoo.

GRANGE FARM

STOCK
45 milkers (Guernseys)
CROPS
50 acres of grassland
(A further 50 acres of grass are rented from the Estate)
LABOUR
Ed Grundy (tenant farmer)
Mike Tucker (milk roundsman and dairy processor)
Harry Mason (milk roundsman)
Jazzer McCreary (milk roundsman – part-time)

Bucking the trend to ever-bigger dairy herds, Grange Farm has a small herd whose milk is sold locally. The secret of its financial success is that it has cut out the 'middle men', in this case the processing dairy and the supermarket. The herd was set up in 2006 by the farm's owner **Oliver Sterling**, who was keen that self-employed milkman **Mike Tucker** should have a local product to sell. Oliver employed young **Ed Grundy** initially as herdsman. Following an outbreak of TB in the herd, Oliver decided to sell up, but Mike and Ed persuaded him to let them run the business. Oliver set up Ed with a Farm Business Tenancy, offering him low-interest loans to get him started. Ed has now expanded the herd and is renting extra grassland from **Borchester Land**, owners of the **Estate**.

GRANGE SPINNEY

Not an idyllic rural hideaway but a new(ish) development of twelve executive houses and six 'affordable' homes. Built in 2003 on a few acres of former farmland, it was the first development in **Ambridge** of locally based **Borchester Land**. Most residents are commuters travelling as far as Birmingham each day. Few play much part in village life. Richard and Sabrina Thwaite are exceptions, throwing themselves into village life with gusto. Not everyone is delighted at the contribution from the competitive Sabrina.

GREY GABLES

A Gothic-style country house built during Victorian times, it is now a plush country hotel owned and run by **Caroline** and **Oliver Sterling**. It is, without doubt, one of the foremost hotels in **Borsetshire**, and head chef **Ian Craig** is fast gaining a reputation in gastronomic circles. The comfortable and well-appointed restaurant specialises in English dishes prepared wherever possible from local produce. Under hotel manager **Roy Tucker**, Grey Gables is becoming an increasingly popular choice for weddings, while the adjoining golf club – now owned by **Borchester Land** – attracts visitors at all times of the year. **Lynda Snell** from **Ambridge Hall** is senior receptionist.

TED GRIFFITHS

(Paul Webster)

Peggy **Woolley** met Ted during one of her daily visits to see her husband **Jack** in the Laurels nursing home. Kindly Ted was there visiting his wife Violet who, like Jack, suffered from dementia. Peggy was shocked when, after a few casual meetings at the nursing home, Ted invited her out to lunch. To the ever-loyal Peggy such an act would have seemed like a betrayal of Jack. But when Peggy was later upset at discovering Jack holding hands with Violet, it was Ted who helped her understand that the bond between the two Laurels' residents implied no rejection of their partners. They were simply 'living in the moment', taking comfort where they could. Later Ted – who was active in the local U3A branch – showed Peggy that it was possible to have a life of her own without feeling she was betraying Jack.

CLARRIE GRUNDY

Keeper's Cottage • Born 12.5.54

(Rosalind Adams)

When Clarrie married **Eddie Grundy**, she never expected a life of ease and luxury. And so far she hasn't been disappointed. Clarrie is one of life's workers. When she isn't cooking and cleaning for Eddie and his 89-year-old father **Joe**, she's making yoghurts with **Pat Archer** in the **Bridge Farm** dairy or pulling pints behind the bar in **The Bull**. Even so, she can be relied upon to bake cakes or make sandwiches for any village event. The biggest sadness in Clarrie's life is the on-going feud between her sons **Will** and **Ed**. Both were at one time in love with **Emma**, daughter of **Neil** and **Susan Carter**. Emma married Will and subsequently had his son **George**. When she later moved in with Ed, the rift between the Grundy boys turned into open conflict. With gamekeeper **Will** now settled with his new partner **Nic Hanson**, Clarrie hopes the feuding is over. But now that Emma is pregnant again – this time by Ed – Clarrie can't be sure of anything.

ED GRUNDY

Rickyard Cottage, Brookfield • Born 28.9.84
(Barry Farrimond)

A few years ago no one would have bet much on Ed having a great future in **Ambridge**. He had served community punishments for joyriding and burglary, while his on-off affair with his brother **Will's** wife **Emma** provoked a series of sometimes vicious fights between the two boys. But retired farmer **Oliver Sterling** saw more in young Ed than many in the village. He entrusted the boy – who had grown up on a dairy farm – with running his new herd of Guernseys. Having settled down with Emma – along with **George**, her son from the relationship with Will – Ed was determined to make a success of the job. This he's done, fully justifying Oliver's faith in him. With Oliver's backing, Ed took on the full tenancy of **Grange Farm**, and is now expanding the herd, renting extra land from the **Estate** to support it. With Emma now expecting his first child, things are looking pretty good right now.

EDDIE GRUNDY

Keeper's Cottage • Born 15.3.51

(Trevor Harrison)

The greatest setback in Eddie's life was losing the tenancy of **Grange Farm** following the bankruptcy of his business. Seeing another Grundy – his son **Ed** – back in Grange Farm has been a great consolation. Eddie is one of life's survivors. Without a farm of his own, he manages to make a living by a variety of entrepreneurial activities – milking part-time at **Brookfield**, selling garden gnomes and bagged compost, laying patios and creating garden landscapes for the better-off folk of **Ambridge**. He's also landed himself a part-time job as livestock handler at **Borchester** Cattle Market. Unofficially, Grundy's farmhouse cider seems to sell in the most unlikely places. Recently Eddie and his father **Joe** have gone into the leisure and tourism industry, opening up their little field as a camp site. Any unsuspecting traveller who happens to pitch up there for the night is likely to encounter late-night revelry from Eddie's Cider Club or an early visit from a large Berkshire sow.

EMMA GRUNDY

(née Carter)
Rickyard Cottage, Brookfield • Born 7.8.84
(Emerald O'Hanrahan)

Life has been a lot quieter for Emma since she settled down at Rickyard Cottage with **Ed**, the dairy farmer, and **George**, her son by Ed's older brother **Will**. The rift between the two brothers is far from healed, though it seldom explodes into open conflict as it once did. For this Emma's much relieved. Life might not be easy, but compared with her early life with Ed – in a cold and draughty caravan – this is luxury. And with Ed making a steady income from his small herd, plus Emma's earnings from cleaning at **Brookfield** and working shifts as a waitress in the Orangery at **Lower Loxley**, the family manage to get by. She and Ed are delighted that she's now expecting their baby.

GEORGE GRUNDY

Rickyard Cottage, Brookfield / Casa Nueva
Born 7.4.05
(Rui Thacker)

Young George has always been an amiable little chap – which is just as well given the tempestuous circumstances he was born into. The son of **Will Grundy** – proven by DNA test following his mother **Emma**'s mistaken belief that **Ed** was his father – he became the object of a bitter squabble between the two boys. After a brief and troubled marriage, Emma was divorced from Will and estranged for several years from Ed. Now Emma and Ed are together and for George life is far quieter. He still spends regular time with Will, who is slowly introducing him to the rich and fascinating life of the gamekeeper. Whether George will one day take up the profession of his father is open to question. George started primary school in September 2009.

JOE GRUNDY

Keeper's Cottage • Born 18.9.21
(Edward Kelsey)

Joe was forced into retirement when he and his son **Eddie** lost the tenancy of **Grange Farm** through bankruptcy. Now his grandson **Ed** is back as tenant of Grange Farm – well most of the land anyway – Joe couldn't be happier. Not that the word retirement seems to have much relevance to Joe. He's still very much involved in village affairs – everything from pantos in the Village Hall to keeping the garden tidy round at **Kathy Perks**'s April Cottage next door. Joe gets around on his pony trap with Bartleby between the shafts. His penchant for turning an easy penny – for example, by selling teas, cider and handmade corn dollies from his field on Open Farm Sunday – has got him into a number of scrapes. Just lately he has struck up an unlikely friendship with **Jim Lloyd**, **Kenton Archer**'s backer in the refurbished **Jaxx Bar**.

WILLIAM GRUNDY

Casa Nueva • Born 9.2.83
(Philip Molloy)

A countryman to his very soul, Will Grundy is every inch the dedicated gamekeeper. Since returning from temporary exile in Gloucestershire – where he fled to escape the relationship tangle involving his ex-wife **Emma** and her new partner, Will's brother **Ed** – he has thrown himself into improving the **Estate** shoot on behalf of his employers, **Borchester Land**. One of his aims – apart from giving clients good sport – is to increase the population of native grey partridges on his home ground, something he's achieving some early success with. After the trouble of the recent past, Will is more settled, enjoying the time he spends with his young son **George**, and happy living with his partner **Nic Hanson** and her children **Jake** and **Mia**. However, Will still harbours a deep resentment towards his brother, one which ignites into anger from time to time.

GRUNDY'S FIELD

A green and pleasant land it isn't. Rather 3.4 acres of rutted pasture-land on which there's a decrepit pole barn, a battered shipping container (which doubles as **Eddie**'s cider store), an ageing tractor, a digger, plus assorted bits of rusting farm equipment. Then there are the heaps of bagged compost, garden gnomes and other ornaments. In the weeks leading up to Christmas the barn rings to the sound of turkeys, and there's usually a pig or two rootling around in the mud. This is the heart of Eddie Grundy's rural business empire and general pottering around field for his father **Joe**. Recently the Grundys came up with a new money-making wheeze for their little corner of England – a camping field. Following a general tidying up, the field is now available for overnight camping. Entertainment at the on-site Cider Club comes free, though not the cider. But there's a good chance you'll get an early awakening from a bunch of weaner pigs.

DR DEEPAK GUPTA

Tettenhall, Wolverhampton

(Madhav Sharma)

A qualified doctor, **Usha**'s father was one of thousands of Ugandan Asians forcibly expelled from the country in 1972. For years this traditionalist patrician disapproved of his daughter's life in **Ambridge** and kept well away. He was content to let Usha's brother **Shiv** and her auntie **Satya Khanna** visit to maintain the family links. Like others in the family, he was particularly upset by Usha's decision to marry Ambridge vicar **Alan Franks**. Shortly before the wedding, the cunning Satya engineered a meeting between father and daughter. Though it was a difficult encounter, Dr Gupta was impressed by Alan's willingness to embrace a full Hindu wedding ceremony as well as a Christian one.

SHIV GUPTA

Coventry
(Shiv Grewal)

Usha Franks's elder brother played a key role in getting the family to accept her choice of a Church of England vicar for her husband. He was best man at her wedding to **Alan Franks**. An accountant by profession, Shiv is something of a gourmet. Only an occasional visitor to Ambridge, he has yet to find a restaurant in the county that really excites his taste buds.

NICOLA (NIC) HANSON

Casa Nueva • Born 1980

(Becky Wright)

With her two youngsters, **Jake** (6) and **Mia** (4) – both by her former partner Andrew – she has brought warmth and laughter into **Casa Nueva**, the gamekeeper's cottage. This is the second time Nic and **Estate** head keeper **Will Grundy** have got it together. On the first occasion the relationship came to an abrupt end when Will caught her smacking his little son **George** and accused her of abuse. Nic, who had reacted spontaneously during a squabble between George and Mia, was outraged by the accusation and promptly went back to her mum's in **Borchester**. Will later regretted his hasty action and wooed her back to **Ambridge**. He helped her pass her driving test so she was no longer reliant on rural buses. She has also been able to take a part-time job in **The Bull**, where her help was crucial during the weeks following Sid Perks's death. Regulars comment that she's 'a natural' behind the bar, but when Will hears them he can't help feeling a nagging pang of jealousy.

JAKE AND MIA HANSON

Casa Nueva • Born 2004 and 2006

(Charles Thorp and Molly Thorp)

Nicola Hanson's two children by her former partner Andrew are the principal reason why there's a lot more laughter around the gamekeeper's cottage than there has been for years. The two happy youngsters have adapted well to country life and now both go to Loxley Barrett Primary School. Both get on well with their stepbrother **George Grundy**.

BUNTY AND REG HEBDEN

Bunty born 20.2.22

(Bunty – Sheila Allen)

The parents of **Shula**'s first husband Mark Hebden and the grandparents of their son **Daniel Hebden Lloyd**. The retired solicitor and his wife had their own definite ideas about how the boy should be educated and it didn't include the local state schools. Shula's present husband **Alistair Lloyd**, who has adopted Daniel, fought a vigorous campaign in favour of state education, but Reg and Bunty got their way and Daniel now attends **Felpersham** Cathedral School.

PATRICK HENNESSEY

(Joseph Kloska)

He works for **Borchester** Wildlife Trust and is a good friend of **Kirsty Miller**, who he met in **Ambridge Organics**. He is the principal reason that she has become a volunteer worker at Arkwright Lake wildlife reserve.

HOLLERTON JUNCTION

A quiet country station that somehow escaped the axe of Dr Beeching in the 1960s. For years the station was much loved by rural ramblers from **Borchester** and quietly loathed by commuters. With grass growing at the ends of the platforms and the once well-tended flower beds overrun with weeds, it hardly looked the model of a modern transport system. With the rise in commuter travel, the station's fortunes have picked up in recent years. The railway company have spruced up the waiting room and extended the times when the ticket office is manned. There are those like **Jim Lloyd** who claim that in an era of rising oil prices, rural railways are about to enter a new golden age. Hollerton Junction stands ready.

HOME FARM

280 ewes (early lambing) • 110 hinds, stags, calves

CROPS
1,118 acres cereals • 148 acres grassland
158 acres oilseed rape • 36 acres linseed
80 acres woodland • 10 acres willow (game cover)
4 acres strawberries • 6 acres maize

OTHER
25-acre riding course • Fishing lake • Maize maze

LABOUR
Adam Macy (managing) • **Debbie Aldridge** (managing)
Andy, Jeff (general workers) • **William Grundy** (gamekeeper)
Pete (assistant keeper) • Students and seasonal labour
Fly (sheepdog)

With 1,585 mainly arable acres, Home Farm is the largest in **Ambridge** and carries out contract farming for **Brookfield**, the **Estate** and other local farms. As a partner in the Hassett Hills Meat Company, it raises and supplies high-quality lamb to butchers and caterers, with **Jennifer** selling its venison and strawberries at local farmers' markets. Adam is currently developing a new cherry enterprise.

CLIVE HORROBIN

In one of Her Majesty's prisons • Born 9.11.72
(Alex Jones)

It remains a mystery how an ordinary family in a leafy English village can produce such a persistent offender as Clive. In his time he's been found guilty of an armed robbery on the village post office, a string of burglaries in the south **Borsetshire** area, and a vicious vendetta against gamekeeper and former policeman George Barford, which ended in the firebombing of George's house. For the second time in his life, Clive sought refuge with his sister **Susan Carter**. She had made the mistake of harbouring him following the post office robbery, an error for which she was given a prison sentence of her own. Following the firebombing incident, however, she turned him in and he's now serving a sentence of twelve years. To this day, Susan wonders how her brother managed to go so wrong.

THE HORROBINS

While **Clive** is the only member of the family who can be classed as a big-time criminal, none of the others – except perhaps the long-suffering **Ivy** – have entirely escaped the eyes of the law. While former council highways worker Bert was busy drinking and gambling his money away, his offspring Keith, Gary, Tracy and Stewart were all making a name for themselves in the magistrate's court. Only **Susan** seemed determined enough to make a clean break from this life on the edge of legality. She married the upright pigman **Neil Carter** and did her best to distance herself from the rest of the family. Sadly for her, she was only partially successful. Her brother Clive did his best to drag her down when he persuaded her to harbour him following his armed raid on the village post office. For this act of misplaced family loyalty, Susan herself was given a prison sentence.

MAURICE HORTON

Borchester

(Philip Fox)

Butcher Maurice came to **Ambridge** to work part-time making sausages for **Tom Archer** at one of the business units at Sawyer's Farm. It was a move that helped him turn his life around. The grumpy butcher had already lost his wife, son and business through compulsive gambling. When Tom approached him, his second business – a shop in **Felpersham** – was about to go under. Making sausages for Tom – and supplementing his income by butchering venison carcasses for **Home Farm** and working part-time in a local supermarket – gave him the space to rebuild his life. When another Ambridge resident with a compulsion for gambling – vet **Alistair Lloyd** – turned up at the **Borchester** branch of Gamblers Anonymous – Maurice was able to give something back by becoming Alistair's sponsor.

JAXX BAR

With its funky wall art and eclectic music styles, the latest and – according to manager **Kenton Archer** – the coolest venue in **Borchester** opened with much razzmatazz in 2010. For Kenton, who had run the place in its earlier manifestation as a café, it was the culmination of a long-held dream. He had resisted the pressure from his chief backer **Jim Lloyd** to turn it into a 'more sophisticated, jazz-orientated' venue, a description Kenton interpreted as a place for oldies. Instead this was to be for the young glitterati of Borchester. So determined was Kenton to be around for the official opening that he declined to accompany his partner **Kathy Perks** to the funeral of her ex-husband, popular pub licensee Sid Perks in New Zealand. It was the decision that made his already strained relationship with Kathy even worse. The couple separated.

SATYA KHANNA

Wolverhampton

(Jamila Massey)

Usha **Franks**'s Auntie Satya became something of a go-between when Usha's parents ended direct contact with their daughter following her move to the countryside. When Satya learned of her niece's attachment to a Christian minister – **Ambridge** vicar **Alan Franks** – she, like the rest of the family, was vehemently opposed to the relationship. However, when Usha started to feel threatened by hostility from the Asian community, Satya came to her rescue, resolutely defending her niece. When Usha and Alan decided to wed, it was Satya who became the prime mover in arranging the Hindu side of the ceremony. Perhaps because of this, Usha is today closer to her aunt than ever. Yet there will always be a side of this modern professional woman that rejects the controlling influence of Satya – such as when her aunt attempted to become a match-maker for then-single Usha. But after the momentous events of the past couple of years she now sees her as a trusted and loyal friend.

ALISTAIR LLOYD

The Stables • Born 1962

(Michael Lumsden)

Alistair's life hasn't got any easier since his father **Jim** came to live in the village. For a while Jim took delight in winding up Alistair's wife **Shula**, a hobby which did little to promote peace and harmony at **The Stables**. Recently Jim has discovered new pastimes such as becoming a team leader in the running of **Ambridge**'s newly established **Community Shop**, and investing money in his business partner Don Sandland's new venture, **Jaxx Bar**, managed by **Kenton Archer**. All of which is good news for Alistair, who doesn't ask a lot more from life than for his clients to pay their vet bills on time, a successful Single Wicket competition in cricket (he's the organiser), plus the odd evening sampling Shire's bitter in the pub. Fortunately he seems to have kicked his gambling habit which probably put more strain on the marriage than night time call-outs and Ambridge cricket combined.

DANIEL HEBDEN LLOYD

The Stables • Born 14.11.94

(Louis Hamblett)

The son **Shula** had with her first husband, Mark Hebden, who died in a car crash. Daniel attends **Felpersham** Cathedral School against the wishes of his father by adoption, **Alistair Lloyd**. Mark's parents **Bunty** and **Reg** are paying for the education. Now in his mid teens, Daniel has started challenging many of his parents' rules and assumptions, a rebellion fuelled by Alistair's father **Jim**. It was Jim who allowed him to take the wheel of his classic Riley car (off-road, of course). This was an adventure too far for Shula and Alistair, who ruled the car off-limits to Daniel in future. When Shula's father Phil became interested in astronomy and bought a telescope, Daniel became fascinated in the subject. When Phil died, he bequeathed the telescope to his grandson ensuring that the boy will spend a fair bit of time gazing heavenward in the future.

JIM LLOYD

Greenacres

(John Rowe)

Vet **Alistair Lloyd** can hardly be said to have been overjoyed when his father, a retired academic, decided to move down from Scotland and spend his final years in **Ambridge**. The relationship between father and son had never been a close one. Now settled, Jim seems determined to make the most of his retirement years. Having bought and settled into Greenacres on the site of the former police house, he drives around the place in an impossibly unreliable Riley car and is a prime mover in **Kenton**'s café-bar project. He has also volunteered to be a team leader in the **Ambridge Community Shop**. Despite these worthy endeavours, there's a distinct touch of the anarchist about Jim, which may be why he counts the irascible **Joe Grundy** amongst his pals. The two of them can be relied upon to lampoon all that's false and deluded about village life. In Ambridge they're never likely to be short of targets.

SHULA HEBDEN LLOYD

(formerly Hebden, née Archer)
The Stables • Born 8.8.58
(Judy Bennett)

It hasn't been a wonderful year for Shula. The recession has taken a sizeable slice of business at the riding stables she runs and, sadly, her father Phil died. All at a time when Shula continued to feel separated from the village church where she had been churchwarden for many years. As she drives to **Felpersham** for the weekly service in the cathedral, she must reflect on the events that led to her resignation as churchwarden – the ill-judged comments made to a journalist about the planned marriage of vicar **Alan Franks** to a Hindu. Perhaps because of her sense of separation from one pillar of village life, she has volunteered to be a team leader in the new **Community Shop**. She'll be working with her father-in-law **Jim**, who has scarcely missed an opportunity to annoy her since coming to live in **Ambridge**. It'll be a testing time, but she's sure to find an inner strength to see her through.

LOWER LOXLEY HALL

The residence of the Pargetter family for generations, this minor stately home has been reinvented as a conference, wedding and family entertainment centre. Among current attractions are a treetop walk, a rare breeds farm, a café, shop and art gallery. In addition there are seven acres of woodland and three acres of formal gardens. Its appeal as a conference and wedding venue is enhanced by an impressive Great Dining Room, Jacobean fireplace and neo-classical library. The whole enterprise is run by the owner **Nigel Pargetter** and his wife **Elizabeth**, and many of the events reflect their own personal interests. There are regular falconry courses and the venue hosts an annual point-to-point. There are also vines producing Lower Loxley's own wine. Staff include ancient retainers Edgar and Eileen Titcombe, volunteer guide **Bert Fry** and catering manager **Lorna Gibbs**. **Hayley Tucker** runs activity visits for schoolchildren, and **Emma Grundy** is a waitress in the Orangery.

ADAM MACY

Honeysuckle Cottage • Born 22.6.67

(Andrew Wincott)

Adam's responsible for the day-to-day running of the biggest farming business in **Ambridge**. He's joint manager of the 1,585-acre **Home Farm** which also farms the 1,020-acre former Berrow **Estate** on contract for the owners, **Borchester Land**. Adam's partner in the enterprise is his half-sister **Debbie**, who spends most of her time in Hungary managing the family farming interests in Eastern Europe. This is probably a good thing since Adam doesn't take kindly to Debbie interfering, as he sees it, in the daily decision-making, though she still manages to do this by email. Having spent time in Africa working on development projects, Adam has his own clear views on the future of agriculture. As well as taking advantage of the support system, he sees the need to grow cash-generating food crops such as protected strawberries. Apart from his interest in Ambridge Cricket Club, Adam works long hours which doesn't always go down well with his civil partner **Ian Craig**.

KATE MADIKANE

(née Aldridge)
Johannesburg • Born 30.9.77
(Kellie Bright)

When Kate called from her home in South Africa to announce that she was coming back to **Borsetshire** to take a course in International Development Studies at **Felpersham** University, her mum **Jennifer** couldn't help but feel anxious. In her younger days, Jennifer and **Brian** used to wonder if she'd ever settle down. The wild young hippie was expelled from school and later took off with a group of travellers. Her first child **Phoebe** was born in a tepee at Glastonbury Festival. Phoebe now lives happily with her father, **Roy Tucker**, stepmother **Hayley** and half-sister **Abbie** in **Ambridge**. Until her sudden return to Ambridge, Kate seemed settled in Johannesburg where she lived with her husband **Lucas**, daughter Noluthando (born 2001) and son Sipho (born 2007). Jennifer now worries about what may lie behind her decision to spend a year at Felpersham University.

LUCAS MADIKANE

Johannesburg • Born 1972

(Connie M'Gadzah)

When journalist Lucas took a job with the South African Broadcasting Corporation in Johannesburg, everyone knew it would be a wrench for his wife **Kate** to move away from the pleasant surroundings of Cape Town. But the couple, with their two children, appear to have made the move successfully and settled down in their new neighbourhood. Lucas seemed to have had a calming influence on this once footloose English girl. Now Kate has left Lucas and the family – she says temporarily – to take a course in International Development Studies at **Felpersham** University in **Borsetshire**. The children will be looked after by Lucas's parents and she'll visit during her holidays. Lucas appears relaxed about it – at least as far as **Jennifer** can tell on the phone. But knowing Kate, Jennifer can't help wondering if there isn't more to it.

HARRY MASON

Ambridge
(Michael Shelford)

When Harry the new milkman arrived in **Ambridge**, everyone thought he seemed a pretty good guy – everyone except **Jazzer McCreary**, that is. For the cynical, tough-talking Glaswegian with a liking for one too many lagers, this amiable, clean-living colleague with scarcely a bad word to say about anyone was just too good to be true. And when this paragon started attracting glances from some of the fittest women in the village, it was almost more than Jazzer could take. Harry even managed to ingratiate himself with **Fallon Rogers**, once the object of Jazzer's desires. She invited the new milkman to stay temporarily at **The Bull** while her mum, the licensee **Jolene Rogers** was away. This would allow Harry to qualify as 'local', she explained, and thus be eligible for the Single Wicket cricket competition. When landlord Sid Perks died in New Zealand and Jolene lost all interest in the pub, Harry proved a tower of strength in support of Fallon as she tried to take on the responsibility herself.

JAZZER McCREARY

Meadow Rise, Borchester • Born 1984

(Ryan Kelly)

This hard-living Glaswegian with the rasping accent brought a certain rawness to this genteel village community in middle England. It seemed to go down pretty well for some of the young women on his early morning milk round, or so it would seem from his stories. But the legend wasn't always borne out by the facts. **Mike Tucker**, who runs the **Grange Farm** dairy business, heard that **Harry**, the clean-cut new milkman, was proving as popular as Jazzer. And **Fallon Rogers**, the pub licensee's daughter and one-time object of Jazzer's desires, admitted to liking him, but that's all. It was quite a blow, he confided later to organic farmer **Tom Archer** whose pigs he looks after part-time. But Jazzer isn't one to worry for long about why any particular young woman hasn't succumbed to his charms. He's soon back strutting his stuff in the clubs of **Borchester.**

KIRSTY MILLER

Borchester

(Anabelle Dowler)

Good-natured Kirsty works in **Helen Archer**'s shop – **Ambridge Organics** – and also in the lively **Jaxx Bar**. In the shop she has been a rock to Helen, helping her cope with special events at a time when pregnancy – by donor insemination – is sapping some of her energy. Through it all, the loyal Kirsty has been there to listen and share in the emotion. Kirsty would be the first to admit that her own life has been rather downbeat in comparison. Recently, however, she has been seeing something of **Patrick Hennessey** who works for **Borchester** Wildlife Trust. But the interest, she insists, is purely ornithological.

PAUL MORGAN

(Michael Fenton Stevens)

Matt Crawford's half-brother turned up unexpectedly at the Dower House during Matt's enforced detention as a guest of Her Majesty. Paul, who had hoped to persuade Matt to visit his sick mother before she died, was immediately attracted to the lonely **Lilian**. She for her part, warmed to Paul's kindness and gentleness. He was, in short, everything that Matt wasn't. Lilian might easily have embarked on a passionate affair with Paul, a possibility not exactly discouraged by her sister **Jennifer**. But Lilian drew back at the bedroom door (of a hotel), later explaining to Paul that she loved Matt too much to hurt him this way.

ELIZABETH PARGETTER

(née Archer)
Lower Loxley Hall • Born 21.4.67
(Alison Dowling)

The hard-headed business side of the partnership with her husband **Nigel** running **Lower Loxley Hall**. While Nigel follows his dreams – some might say his whims – clear-thinking Elizabeth can be relied upon to keep a firm grasp on reality. There's undoubtedly a ruthless side to Elizabeth, as her brother **David** discovered a few years back when she contested the inheritance arrangements over the family farm, **Brookfield**. The rift with David has never fully healed. More recently she has been critical of his handling of his daughter **Pip**'s relationship with the much older **Jude Simpson**. In her mother **Jill**'s view, Elizabeth needed a certain doggedness to get through. She was born with a congenital heart defect and, following the birth of her twins **Lily** and **Freddie**, needed a heart valve replacement operation. But she has always been the power behind the Lower Loxley business, and nothing's likely to change this.

LILY AND FREDDIE PARGETTER

Lower Loxley Hall • Born 12.12.99

(Georgie Feller and Jack Firth)

Despite the challenges of running **Lower Loxley Hall**, **Elizabeth** makes sure she makes plenty of space in her day for the twins. Perhaps because their mother's heart problems led to concerns around the time of their birth, the two are especially loved. Some would think them very lucky to be growing up at Lower Loxley with its boundless green spaces and constant exciting events.

NIGEL PARGETTER

Lower Loxley Hall • Born 8.6.59
(Graham Seed)

Despite the financial downturn, **Lower Loxley Hall** continues to be a success, which is a surprise to many who know Nigel. His recent 'crazes' have included a restored ha-ha, a memorial to his great-uncle Rupert, and a planet-saving decision to travel everywhere by bike. The family home is now insulated with sheep's wool, heated by woodchip boiler and offers 'green weddings'. There's also a Lower Loxley vintage wine. Thanks to the steadying hand of his wife **Elizabeth** on the tiller, the place still manages to stay in profit. Nigel's latest venture is allotments, which he plans to lease long-term to locals. There's been something of an upheaval with Elizabeth's brother **Kenton** moving in at short notice having walked out on his partner **Kathy Perks**. Nigel's determination to support Kenton through this difficult time gets him into trouble, including a brush with the law.

JAMIE PERKS

April Cottage • Born 20.7.95
(Dan Ciotkowski)

Jamie, who lives with his mother **Kathy Perks**, suffered a great shock when his father, Sid Perks, died suddenly in New Zealand. Kathy and Sid were divorced and Sid, the landlord of **The Bull**, was living with his new wife **Jolene**. But Jamie saw a lot of his father and the death came as a great loss. Jamie sought consolation from Kathy's then-boyfriend, **Kenton Archer**, and from his friend, young **Josh Archer** at **Brookfield**. When Kathy and Kenton split up over the stress of recent events, Jamie retreated into himself. Angry and confused, he trashed the new bird hide at Arkwright Lake with friends. The future looks bleak.

JOLENE PERKS

(née Rogers)
The Bull
(Buffy Davis)

The former country singer – one-time Lily of Layton Cross – reinvented herself as the archetypal landlady of a country pub. But the untimely death of her beloved husband Sid, long-time landlord of **The Bull**, changed her mind about it. Basically she wanted nothing to do with the place. As a result the once popular pub went rapidly downhill. Though regulars remained loyal, the ambience was far from welcoming. Anxious to dissuade her mother from putting the pub on the market, **Fallon Rogers** threw herself into getting the business back on course. Touched by her daughter's efforts, Jolene responded by making an effort to raise her game. But her continuing sadness has placed a large question mark over the pub's long-term future.

KATHY PERKS

(formerly Holland)
April Cottage • Born 30.1.53
(Hedli Niklaus)

Though Kathy and Sid had been divorced for a number of years, his death hit her particularly hard. It was her boyfriend **Kenton Archer**'s refusal to accompany her and son **Jamie** to Sid's funeral in New Zealand (Kenton decided instead to stay at home for the grand opening of the new **Jaxx Bar**) that put an added strain on their relationship. Kenton accompanied Kathy to the annual dinner dance at **Ambridge Golf Club** where she works but he drank too much, so Kathy had to drive him home early. The next day there was a row and Kenton walked out, moving temporarily to his sister **Elizabeth**'s little pad, **Lower Loxley Hall**. Kathy was sad when Jamie blamed her for the bust-up. But when she heard that Kenton had boasted about a drunken encounter with the police, she began to think that she and Jamie were better off without him. It seems doubtful whether she and Kenton can ever get back together.

HEATHER PRITCHARD

Prudhoe, Northumberland

(Joyce Gibbs)

Because she lives so far from **Ambridge**, **Ruth Archer**'s mum doesn't get the chance to visit her grandchildren – **Pip**, **Josh** and **Ben** – as often as she'd like. Widowed several years ago, she has an active social life at home in Prudhoe, and is sufficiently well off to take a cruise whenever she feels the need to recharge her batteries. However, she likes nothing better than visiting **Brookfield** and catching up with the friends she has made over the years. Among them is **Alistair Lloyd**'s father **Jim**. She was very fond of Phil and his death came as a shock.

FALLON ROGERS

The Bull • Born 19.6.85

(Joanna van Kampen)

The singer in the band the Little White Lies has seen her music career slow down of late. This is good news for the regulars of **The Bull** as it means that the popular promoter of music nights 'Upstairs@The Bull' spends a good bit of time behind the bar these days. There she met **Harry Mason**, the new milkman, and immediately hit it off with him. She invited him to stay at the pub for a while so he would qualify as a local resident and thus be eligible for the Ambridge Cricket Club Single Wicket competition. Some of the regulars thought the explanation a little unlikely. **Jazzer McCreary**, who once held a torch for Fallon, thought it downright implausible. He was even crosser when Harry went on to win the competition. Like her mum **Jolene**, Fallon was deeply upset by the death of Sid. She hopes her mum will decide to stay in the village and carry on running The Bull.

GRAHAM RYDER

Borchester
(Malcolm McKee)

A land agent working for the **Borchester** firm of Rodways, Graham used to spend a fair bit of his working week in **Ambridge**. Rodways were responsible for running the **Estate** on behalf of **Borchester Land**, and Graham used to work from the Estate office. Then **Matt Crawford** passed the management responsibility to **Debbie Aldridge**, and Rodways were no longer required. These days Graham spends most of his time managing commercial property in town. But he can't entirely get Ambridge out of his system. He once tried to get the village panto closed down by invoking health and safety regulations. It's unlikely that his employers were delighted with his actions. Any chance they may have had of winning back the Estate contract will hardly have been improved by their employee's flat-footed intervention.

ANNABELLE SCHRIVENER

Felpersham

(Julia Hills)

The senior partner of a law firm specialising in property, Annabelle is on the board of **Borchester Land** where she provides legal advice and occasionally a bit of Machiavellian scheming. Originally brought onto the board by **Matt Crawford**, she worked with **Brian Aldridge** on a strategy to get Matt deposed when it became clear that his private financial dealings were about to lead to an action for fraud. Annabelle shares Brian's aim of taking BL into the big league with a few choice land development projects. Brian sees her as a key to attaining his ambitions. Her undoubted legal talents – combined with her readiness to use her considerable charms to win over the opposition – make her a formidable ally. Annabelle's strong competitive streak shows through even in her leisure activities. She likes to run and is an enthusiastic entrant in the **Felpersham** Marathon.

SILENT CHARACTERS

These are the band of characters who, over the years, have stamped their personalities on **Ambridge** without their voices having ever been heard. The current group include Mrs Potter and Mr Pullen at Manorfield Close; the Titcombes – Edgar and Eileen – who are gardener and housekeeper at **Lower Loxley**; Jessica, Lower Loxley's resident falconer; Pete, the under-keeper on the **Estate** shoot; Ronnie Grant, **Christopher Carter**'s farrier boss; **Home Farm** staff Andy and Jeff; **Eddie Grundy**'s friends Baggy and Fat Paul; bell-ringer Neville Booth and his nephew Nathan; Leigh Barham, director of golf at **Ambridge Golf Club**; Richard and Sabrina Thwaite; the Buttons; Derek Fletcher, former chair of the parish council and village busybody; a number of **Horrobins**; the ever-popular cook at **The Bull**, Freda Fry; Rhys Evans, the Welsh barman now helping at **The Bull** since Sid Perks's untimely death, and Rosemary Hopwood, **Lily** and **Freddie's** private tutor at Lower Loxley.

JUDE SIMPSON

Borchester

(Piers Wehner)

A web design student from **Borchester** College, Jude's romance with **Pip Archer** – ten years his junior – was the cause of much disquiet at **Brookfield**, particularly on the part of **David**, her father. He was outraged. He only needed an excuse to ban Jude from Brookfield, and he got it when Jude's reckless driving of the farm's quad bike led to Pip bashing her head and having to be taken to the local hospital's A & E unit. The ban had little effect, though. As **Ruth** pointed out, it was counterproductive since Pip promptly began sleeping over at **Lower Loxley Hall**, home of her Aunt **Elizabeth**. Jude continued to show little consideration for her. He even persuaded her to go clubbing the night before an important exam. He soon tired of her. He packed up college and went off on a trip to the States, telling Pip they were finished. Pip was devastated. While sympathetic, David and Ruth were relieved to get their daughter back.

CORIANDER AND LEONIE SNELL

Born 1974 and 1975

(Alexandra Lilley and Sara Poyzer)

Robert **Snell**'s two daughters by his first marriage. Coriander, known as 'Cas', had a baby boy – Oscar – in 2009, giving much delight to Robert and 'step-grandma' **Lynda** when the two girls plus Oscar came to stay at **Ambridge Hall**.

LYNDA SNELL

Ambridge Hall • Born 29.5.47

(Carole Boyd)

With boundless energy, Lynda plays a part in pretty well everything that goes on in **Ambridge**. While holding down the job of senior receptionist at **Grey Gables**, and, with husband **Robert**, running her own B & B enterprise at **Ambridge Hall**, she's also taken a lead in setting up the **Community Shop** and steering through the tricky proposal for a green burial site in Ambridge. Lynda's passion is the performing arts. At Christmas she usually brings her theatrical talents to bear on the village panto. In 2010, she notched up another first for Ambridge: a murder mystery enacted as part of the village fete. With script written by Lynda, the intriguing title was 'The Strange Affair at Ambridge Towers'. Perhaps, amid all this activity, Lynda is trying to forget some underlying sadness, but, whatever the motivation, most villagers would say they have a real asset in Lynda. Recently she has been taking delight in her 'step-grandson', baby Oscar, son of Robert's daughter **Coriander**.

ROBERT SNELL

Ambridge Hall • Born 5.4.43

(Graham Blockey)

Having run his own software business, Robert has now embarked upon a late second career as **Ambridge**'s resident handyman. He'll turn his hand to pretty well everything from fitting a new kitchen to fitting out and decorating the new **Community Shop**. At home in **Ambridge Hall**, he's the chief greeter and cook in the B & B enterprise as well as being cheerleader for his wife **Lynda** and her many enterprises. He has two daughters from a first marriage – **Leonie** and **Coriander**, who last year presented him with a baby grandson, Oscar. Without doubt Lynda is the greatest love in Robert's life, but he's also very fond of cricket.

ST STEPHEN'S CHURCH

Consecrated 1281

The death of longstanding organist **Phil Archer** marked the end of an era for this beautiful church. Several generations of Archers were already buried in the churchyard. Another Archer – **Shula Hebden-Lloyd** – severed her close connection with the church when she resigned as a churchwarden following the controversial marriage of vicar **Alan Franks** to a Hindu, **Usha** Gupta. It seems fitting that one of the two new wardens at St Stephen's is a member of the Archer family – **Christine Barford**, née Archer. For all the controversies – women vicars and church toilets included – St Stephen's continues to attract a sizeable congregation, which makes it rather different from many village churches today. Alan Franks, with his one hundred per cent commitment – must be part of the reason.

THE STABLES

The home and business of **Shula Hebden Lloyd**, who bought it in 2001 from her aunt, **Christine Barford**. The recession has had a damaging effect on the business, with revenues from both the livery and the riding school substantially down on a couple of years ago. Shula and her husband **Alistair Lloyd** are relieved to have the income from Alistair's veterinary practice, which he runs from the site.

CAROLINE STERLING

(née Bone, formerly Pemberton)
Grange Farm • Born 3.4.55
(Sara Coward)

With her aristocratic connections, Caroline is the perfect host at the classy country hotel, **Grey Gables**. She first ran it on behalf of the then owner, **Jack Woolley**, who delighted in having such a well-connected manager. After tragically losing her first husband Guy Pemberton only six months into their marriage, she made a match with fellow hunting enthusiast, **Oliver Sterling**, who owned **Grange Farm**. Together they bought Grey Gables, so Caroline now owns the business that she has spent so long looking after. The recession has not made things easy in the past couple of years. But with the help of talented staff – including general manager **Roy Tucker** and head chef **Ian Craig** – Caroline has managed to weather the storm. She would be the first to admit that she couldn't have done it without the support and active help of Oliver.

OLIVER STERLING

Grange Farm
(Michael Cochrane)

When Oliver sold his large farm and bought **Grange Farm** in **Ambridge**, he was planning an active retirement including plenty of hunting plus a bit of hobby farming on his 50 acres. He attracted a good deal of hostility from **Eddie Grundy**, the previous occupier of Grange Farm, who had lost his tenancy as a result of bankruptcy. But when Oliver offered young **Ed Grundy** the job of managing his small herd of Guernsey cows, Eddie quickly changed his attitude. What had been planned as a hobby farm quickly became a serious business, supplying milk to local milkman **Mike Tucker**. Having launched the business, Oliver decided to move on, selling the cows to Ed and setting him up as the tenant of Grange Farm. Now Oliver has more time to help his wife **Caroline** run **Grey Gables**. He has also become one of seven team leaders managing the **Community Shop**.

MABEL THOMPSON

Bradford

(Mona Hammond)

The mother of vicar **Alan Franks**'s deceased first wife Catherine, Mabel is a woman of strong views, most of them informed by her evangelical Christian faith. Alan's engagement and subsequent marriage to **Usha** Gupta, a Hindu, was too radical a step for her to accept. Her opposition to the marriage caused much upset at the vicarage and soured her relationship with granddaughter **Amy**. The rift has largely been healed: the essentially warm-hearted Mabel has now accepted the marriage, realising that it is based on deep love and respect. She continues to see it as her duty to support Alan in his ministry, and if that includes accepting Usha as the vicar's wife, she is prepared to go along with it. However, Mabel's occasional visits to **Ambridge** continue to be lively and challenging.

ABIGAIL (ABBIE) TUCKER

Willow Farm • Born 7.3.08

(Daisy Pettifer)

After a difficult birth – **Hayley** went into labour ten weeks early – Abbie came home to **Willow Farm** to be little sister to **Phoebe Aldridge**, the daughter of **Roy Tucker** and **Kate Madikane**, now temporarily back in **Ambridge** from her home in South Africa. The Tuckers – Hayley and **Roy** – are delighted to have a child of their own. Abbie is a happy child who has developed a strong attachment to **Mike Tucker**'s new wife **Vicky**, which is more than some members of the family have.

BRENDA TUCKER

1, The Green • Born 21.1.81
(Amy Shindler)

A marketing graduate from Felpersham University, Brenda has struggled to find a job at a difficult time. As far as her fiancé **Tom Archer** is concerned this is hardly a problem. With the **Bridge Farm** organic food enterprises doing reasonably well, he'd be more than happy for her to come home and rear babies. Brenda will have none of it. She's determined to carve out a career to match her skills and experience before she settles down to a domestic routine. So determined was she to establish a career that she took a job with a marketing agency in Leicester, a post that involved hours of driving to and from work. She now works close to home as PA to property developers **Lilian Bellamy** and **Matt Crawford**. Tom's not entirely happy about that either. She has worked for Matt before and last time it turned decidedly nasty.

HAYLEY TUCKER

(née Jordan)
Willow Farm • Born 1.5.77
(Lorraine Coady)

A trained nanny, Hayley works at **Lower Loxley Hall** where she runs activities for visiting school parties. She is also mother to **Phoebe** – husband **Roy**'s daughter by **Kate** Aldridge, now **Madikane** – and **Abbie**, the happy conclusion of a long struggle to become pregnant. The family live in the house Roy grew up in – the farmhouse at **Willow Farm**, now converted into two residences. Next door Roy's father **Mike** lives with his new wife **Vicky**. A cheerful Brummie, Hayley reckons life is pretty much how she'd always hoped it would be. There's only one slight niggle to disturb things – Kate's reappearance on the **Ambridge** scene. From past knowledge of Kate and her relationship with Phoebe, she can't help but worry.

MIKE TUCKER

Willow Cottage • Born 1.12.49

(Terry Molloy)

Mike's whirlwind romance and subsequent marriage to **Vicky** seemed over-hasty to some members of the Tucker family, not least to Mike's daughter **Brenda**. She and a fair few other **Ambridge** residents don't think it'll last. But Mike's been blissfully happy. So much so that he readily accepted Vicky's offer to invest in some more Guernsey cows for **Ed**, allowing him to expand the herd and Mike to take on a new milkman to expand the retailing side. What neither he nor Ed bargained for was Vicky becoming actively involved in the running of the farm. So appalled was she that male calves were having to be slaughtered at just a few days old that she insisted Ed reared them on while she developed a local market for veal. Ed resented the interference and told Mike so. Was this the first cloud on Mike's new blissful horizon?

ROY TUCKER

Willow Farm • Born 2.2.78

(Ian Pepperell)

Roy is the popular manager of **Grey Gables**, husband of the attractive and effervescent **Hayley**, and father of their daughter **Abbie** and of **Phoebe**, his child with **Kate Madikane**, formerly Aldridge. They live in half of the farmhouse at **Willow Farm**, next door to his father **Mike** and his second wife **Vicky**. For a lad who was once part of a racist gang that terrorised Asian lawyer **Usha Franks** (née Gupta), Roy has turned out pretty well. Not that he hasn't had setbacks. When he and Kate went their separate ways, he had to fight hard for his right to bring up Phoebe. So the return of Kate to **Ambridge** to do a course at **Felpersham** University is worrying for both him and Hayley. Kate's deepening relationship with Phoebe inevitably puts a strain on Hayley which in turn impacts on Roy and Hayley's marriage. Things won't be quite the same again for the Tucker family.

VICKY TUCKER

(née Hudson)
Willow Cottage
(Rachel Atkins)

Vicky hit **Ambridge** like a whirlwind. First to succumb was **Mike Tucker**, still getting over the death of his wife Betty. Almost before he had time to draw breath, they were married and flinging off their clothes on a nude beach near their honeymoon hideaway. Next she set out to reform agriculture. Not content with lending **Ed Grundy** the money to expand his dairy herd, she insisted on giving the cows names like Topsy and Sophie. Hardly a move likely to impress a wind-burned son of the soil like Ed. Next she decided he needed a new veal calf enterprise so the young calves wouldn't have to be slaughtered at birth. As Ed complained to milkman Mike, who buys his milk, 'If she carries on like this I might as well put her name in place of mine on the farm tenancy agreement.' The response of Mike to this dig at his wife is not recorded.

WAYNE TUCSON

Borchester
(Sion Probert)

This former small-town country singer was once married to **Bull** licensee **Jolene Perks** and is the father of **Fallon Rogers**. When he turned up in **Ambridge** drunk and sleeping rough, kind-hearted Jolene allowed him to stay at the pub, an arrangement that went on for far too long in the opinion of her now deceased husband, Sid. The episode did, however, allow Fallon to bond once more with her father. She is happy about that, but also relieved that he is now living a more settled life in **Borchester**.

ANNETTE TURNER

Born September 1990

(Anne-Marie Piazza)

The younger daughter of Greg, the gamekeeper who committed suicide, she arrived in **Ambridge** when life in France with her mother and the new boyfriend became difficult. In Ambridge, **Helen Archer** – Greg's former girlfriend – found space for her in her flat and offered motherly help and advice. Annette became pregnant after sleeping with Helen's boyfriend. Not knowing who the father was, Helen offered to help bring up the baby. The offer was rejected and Annette had an abortion, a decision which caused great anguish for Helen who was already feeling she wanted a child of her own. Annette then moved out to live with her grandmother, leaving Helen feeling rejected. Soon afterwards, Helen made the decision to have a child by donor insemination.

UNDERWOODS

Borchester's own department store has had to reinvent itself a number of times to keep up with changes in the High Street. But through it all two areas seem to thrive whatever the state of retailing – the Food Hall and the coffee shop. The Food Hall has long had a policy of stocking high quality local foods such as **Bridge Farm** organic yoghurt and ice cream, a policy that is now paying off handsomely. As for the coffee shop, it's known as a better source of local news than the *Borchester Echo* and Radio **Borsetshire** combined.

WILLOW FARM

The farmhouse is split into two. On one side – now called Willow Cottage – **Mike Tucker** lives with his wife **Vicky** amid the bright décor she chose to match the mood of their new marriage. On the other side – and it must be said amid rather more sober colours – Mike's son **Roy** lives with his wife **Hayley** and daughters **Phoebe** and **Abbie**. Nearby are eight acres owned by **Neil Carter**. Neil and his wife **Susan** live in their own self-built house, while alongside is the land where Neil runs his outdoor herd of breeding sows. There's also an organic free-range laying bird enterprise run by Neil in partnership with Hayley.

HAZEL WOOLLEY

LA, New York, Tooting… who knows?
Born 15.2.56
(Annette Badland)

Jack Woolley's adopted daughter claims to be a film director, though no one has ever spotted her name on any credits. She appears occasionally in **Ambridge** usually to get her father to sign over one or other of his property interests to her. Since Jack was hit by Alzheimer's she has had to go through the formidable **Peggy**, so she rarely bothers now.

JACK WOOLLEY

The Lodge, Grey Gables • Born 19.7.19

(Arnold Peters)

Once the most successful businessman in **Ambridge**, Jack is now confined to a care home with advanced dementia. The self-made Brummie, who once owned **Grey Gables**, the country park and golf course, plus the ***Borchester*** *Echo*, now has his affairs managed by his devoted (third) wife **Peggy**. Loyally, Peggy visits him most days, though the response she gets depends largely on what sort of day he's having. Once or twice she has been upset to find Jack holding hands with Violet, another dementia patient in the home. Violet's husband **Ted** – also a regular visitor – explained that he had felt the same hurt about Violet. But he'd been able to let it go knowing that his wife had no comprehension of it.

PEGGY WOOLLEY

(née Perkins, formerly Archer)
The Lodge, Grey Gables • Born 13.11.24
(June Spencer)

Peggy, the plucky East End girl who lived through the London Blitz, has had her share of troubles since coming to **Ambridge**. Her first husband Jack Archer, one-time landlord of **The Bull**, was an alcoholic, hardly a good qualification for the job. Now her second husband – also **Jack** – is in the final stages of Alzheimer's, and the ever-loyal Peggy is having to painfully work out how to take back part of her life as the man she is devoted to is slowly and surely lost to her. Peggy's comfort is the family – especially her children **Jennifer Aldridge**, **Lilian Bellamy** and **Tony Archer**, plus the various grandchildren. To all of them Peggy is a rock – solid, dependable and always ready to help.